ACTION

ACTION

First published in 2014 by Peanut Books
a literary offshoot of punctum books
Brooklyn, NY
http://punctumbooks.com

ISBN-13: 978-0692335543
ISBN-10: 0692335544

Library of Congress Cataloging Data is available from the Library of Congress.

Cover Photo: *D.B. MacMillan*, 1910.
George Grantham Bain Collection,
Library of Congress.

Author photo by Mel Keiser.

I USED TO MAKE THE BIGGEST FEASTS FOR NOBODY.

-L.O.

Peanut Books | Brooklyn, NY

ACTION

[poems]

Anthony Opal

CONTENTS

ACTION

ACTION

dear god-and-a-half dear action painter
dear compassionate sloth and hammerhead
shark who willingly gave up the hammer
dear directionless each and every
direction at once dear homeless zoo
keeper dark inverted sun and broke-
winged finch healed-winged falcon dear
surprising January rain running
quickly from rooftops like prophets' voices
in the wind which brought it to them
not beyond infection or cancer or
arthritis or fevers or doubt but rather
those unseen jet streams howling throughout
the land to break things up again

SLAVE

I take my medication and then fall
in love with a gull the holy slob
that I am its toes dug into the sand
and the other gulls held up by strings
though nothing casts a shadow anymore
on a day like this I want to sing
a song to myself in the silence of
myself something like "dearest bird you are
too much for me to handle I'm not
worthy to untie the thong of your sandal"
and then to imagine this gull wearing
sandals and fall asleep for the first time
happy due to the absurdity of
the very grandeur of a mute being

THE CITRUS-BIRD PROBLEM

only one bird breed lives in lemon trees
until I Googled it and found out
that many bird breeds live in lemon trees
and that it's actually a problem
people have keeping these birds out
of their citrus the worst being the oranges
but then I Googled that and it turns out
the citrus-bird problem is universal
and not a joking matter like last night
when Jake made fun of Jean-Dominique
Bauby by blinking his left eye
and then regretted it or the time when
I took too lightly the citrus-bird problem
that we were having metaphorically

EXODUS ETC

we hung our harps on the poplar trees
growing left-leaning from the muddy banks
of the river our captors demanded
that we sing songs of G-d's good deeds
and faithfulness in times of trouble I saw
a dead bush burst into flames my mind
reeling with hate for each stupid fish-mouth
that came to the surface for air as if
the river cared or the river was fair
which is when Levi stared singing about
the time Moses struck a rock with a stick
and just couldn't get the water to stop

SMALL GOD

and who am I to not slowly fashion
a small god from the fingernail clippings
of the girl I love Jackson Pollock of
the body was an idea I had
for a sculpture imagining if chaos
were spatial like what happens when
a word disappears into an object
between us the vase of your shoulders or
as André Breton put it better
"my wife whose shoulders are champagne"
and then to wake in the myriad mums
(my pubic hair littered with mum pollen)
to Adam's excited utterance
"oh bone of my bone and flesh of my flesh"

BACK ROADS AND WORM HOLES

darkness and diphtheria mix with softness
the shape of a brick-cornered
building encompassing a map of West
Africa (explaining this tit-for-tat
and stray cat moaning as some suffering
is just too much and the only way
to get at it's by back roads and worm holes
the removal of all things to make her
say "okay okay I remember that")
the firefly fat with light swarming inside
the jar to make the center of the palm
bright as the person carrying it I
used to have so much to say before the rain
carried me away and now it steers

LIST

things I would miss upon leaving here
frozen pasta referred to as "the nests"
real sonnets by unreal prophets
pale darkness of the morning our bed
the silence therein noise of the fan
waking in the middle of the night
to take a piss without lights on stumbling
back upstairs glimpsing the snow
the nocturnal crow the possum digging
in the compost bin the laughter of it
inside myself and G-d still unresolved by
hope in ecstacy the Fibonacci
sequence coupled with this reality
of strange mercy that pulls us inward

MECHANICAL
SUNFLOWER

"I hope like a hatchback bird at least
some semblance of worship comes from these"
was supposed to be the last couplet of
this last poem but I couldn't get there and
so decided to start here (with what
gratitude) as I walk through the hospital
lobby and out into the parking lot
leaving behind tubes of blood with
my name on them address and birthday it's
all so odd how someday I'll be just one
petal on the mechanical sunflower
which is why I think she keeps telling me
that for some love leads to discipline
and for others it's the other way around

KING DAVID

no longer allowed inside the temple
I take pills in order to access
the absent G-d shaped door a portico
outside which I wait like King David
at the back of a cave huddled and itching
my chest from withdrawal while having
the wherewithal to withstand it all
I find myself cleaved from innocence
and experience alike remaining alive
solely to coincide with the hell of
"we strive for five" around the corner
where sunlight streaks the streets like water
only more beautiful as sunlight
is able to be displaced by a shadow

THE WAY YOUR T-SHIRT HUNG

dreamt of you but not as a scholar I
couldn't have dreamt anything kinder
or more supple or gentler or smaller
than the curves of an airplane window
(the divot of your bellybutton becoming
a universe to be flipped over like
a cosmetic mirror one side magnified
the other normal) as if it were you
the wife of my youth of apple bearings
and single trees the receding light
plain-old-light inside a plane of light
and how we love to fly I remember
touching down in Sierra Leone the way
your T-shirt hung in the humid air

COMING DOWN THE MOUNTAIN

within the cold impersonal cleft
of G-d in which Moses verily stood
hearing a voice as in a sudden herd
run off the edge of an eastern cliff
to become a stolid solitary blip
on the map a snapped tree's time zone
and then to descend Sinai become old
holding a cup up to deserted lips
an angel wrenching a young man's hip
long ago on the banks of the Jabbok
Moses swings and strikes a rock
cupping water up to deserted lips
within the cold impersonal cleft of G-d
the universe (musical atonal) skips

SCRAWLED LIKE A FILEFISH

alas saying *Yes Yes* this is a good
painting my dynamic crumpled horn is
run into the ground even as my slow
body is covered in layers of shirts
and that's not all she too covers me
when I'm sick and also when I'm not
I feel her nipples where my fingers meet
to become palms cupping a handful
of hair and letting it fall against her
back as sunlight felled by an axe
on the cool bed in the afternoon I
return to my painting with *Yes Yes*
scrawled across the bottom of it like
a filefish (the opposite of habit)

THE COYOTE

I invite the coyote in and give him
free reign of the interior space
to redecorate my place in accordance
with his tastes to which I can't relate
yet am surprisingly excited at
the prospect of hating the color scheme
coyote chooses or the arrangement
of the furniture the hanging artwork
(though we both love Jackson Pollock
and the violence inherent to those
strokes that cross the other ones out)
"I am nature" Pollock says coyote
once told me to which I replied loudly
"I know coyote I know I know"

YOUR BEST OWL SUIT

stick to the image of the owl or the tall
thin pine around the lake imagine
that it was your home and that you were
a collector of squirrel bones watching
them fall end over end from unknown
heights do you think this would change
your views on religion or politics
even though you would never be allowed
to vote or attend a church service
unless you listened from the bell tower
or took communion from a rain puddle
or punched the ballot with your beak you
probably wouldn't care wouldn't put on
your best owl suit wouldn't even own one

ENTERING THE WATER
WITHOUT LOOKING

scaffolding of a butterfly boat
above ten darkly schooling syllables
the body launches from its farthest shore
experiencing all as one layer
among others among the darkness of
a half-dozen objects falling
from our hands as we took off our pants
and hung them from the branches
entering the water without looking
(an airplane passing overhead) it took us
an hour to remember who we were and
how water always appears clearest
from above even though light angles in

NO SNOW IN THE JUNGLE

a paper airplane made of fractals is
thrown into the jungle or at least that's
how it feels to be the jungle I mean
a self-injection of Etanercept
into either "the thigh or the stomach"
is what the nurse says "but first make sure
that the syringe is clear and doesn't
look like a snow globe" which I suppose
means that no snow is allowed in
the jungle that it wouldn't survive
there or accumulate on the jungle floor
or the jungle vines or the jungle
animals (who would surely die) so I
warm it up and sterilize the spot twice

HALLELUJAH TO PORNO-GRAPHIC COLLAGE

geese collapse one after another
into the suburban pond as thunder
sounding a timpani in the distance
rolls in past treble clef lemon trees
with this or that disease I mean
rheumatoid arthritis plus vaccines
for arguing about whether or not
revelation is a thing (so sing
if you don't believe in music and cling
if you don't believe in G-d) a firefly
in the sermon on the mount's *Selah*
hallelujah to pornographic collage
rough sex turned into stained glass like
a tall church in place of a roadmap

*2:00am, hospital, morphine

THE WING'S BODY

the materials of darkness are this
crow's broken wing reflecting daylight
through the middle of the kitchen where
I'm sitting in a chair reclining deeper
into the breast of the last supper
until leaning forward for the first time
in years as whose paternal twin I
envision the lonely wing on the lawn
the body somewhere else just sitting there
it's me I think to myself I must be
missing my left arm always have been
though I'm lying as nothing is ever
always so I'll just mourn for both of us
and start tomorrow as the wing's body

GOOD MORNING

bird beak like a rawhide bone remains
enthroned in the orange flesh of a cantaloupe
alongside the pill on the windowsill
I presently take with a smallish lake
of water pooled at the bottom of
my cup that no longer runneth over
in the morning but rather takes its time
like the blue charcoal sunrise I find
my mind somewhere else between the Pink
Lady apple and the Earl Grey tea
in a white ceramic mug layered steam
like transient feathers falling in reverse
to the sound of elevated trains in
the distance I hear through open windows

WAKING UP TO SNOW

I chase the furry animal until
it ducks into a drainage ditch which
is only me waking up from a dream
the darkness held in spite of the daylight
I've been told by those who claim
to know the will of gods and devils
oh G-d it sure is beautiful here
waking up before the sun begins
the morning pale as an unformed eye
drinking green tea steeping it too long
until it's bitter as hell I add some
milk and honey to take the edge off
realizing that *Christ* it snowed all night
and that the pilot light blew out
the moment that winter hit the garden

JOHN CAGE

a fly is something that exploded
and was put back together in the name
of magnetism's fear or atonal
music and so a fly is like John Cage
or the sort of thing John Cage would sing
if he sang (and he does sing) I mean
secret things composed of a low hum
in the shower or the car in mid-flight
its vibrant wings exploding in the air
in the middle of an open expanse like
how on earth did I ever get here

HALF A BIRD MASK

I wear an unfashionable bird mask
to paint my portrait before the party
as a child in a suit did I mention
it's only half a mask and that my wife
made it for me because I'm unhappy
talking endlessly about poetry
adjusting my stance to wrestle this
angel at Penuel I break its wing
as it dislocates my hip demanding
to know my name to which I say "I
am unfashionable I bathe in the
water naked as the hour I was born"

INVISIBLE PLANE

have you seen the hippo's mouth open
wide its white teeth rise like skyscrapers
from its black gums felt the weight of
a small thing on top of you seen the northern
lights how they shine like the skin
of your thighs stepping from the shower
and reaching for a towel did you see
the green finch just before it hit the window
how it looked like you just before you
hit the window and by you I mean me before
I hit the window that invisible plane
that breaks the line and the man the same

VARIETIES OF WAR

if suffering doesn't bring about
resurrection the longing inherent
to suffering will do it (intuit
a spark a fire Christ nonexistent
for three days not simply
somewhere else in heaven or hell but
in a cave behind a stone a body
without the electricity of a soul
empty zeros of nothingness being
filled up by G-d knows what
cold moments utterly void
of love in the living room or kitchen
the loneliness inherent to this
haplessness of all varieties of war)

STAY

"I want to be here" is the simplest
form of praise I know the ozone levels
are so high today I have a headache
but love the slope of your breasts the way
a bird swoops into the hole in the wall
outside the kitchen window means
we're finally sharing a home I suppose
I could've been more romantic instead
of writing about those other bodies
moving around me like yesterday I saw
this shadow on the floor of the river as
water was brooding dove-like above it

GOLDEN CITY

daylight reconstructs the sign of Jonah
in reverse as each tiny bird in its
tiny hearse wakes up and forsakes
its tiny wings for panes of light the size
of Moby Dick unwounded no longer white
as G-d laughs by the leaves of the trees
they crash into each other with their
new bodies and golden beaks which are
meant to be a joke because gold is so
damn ugly who would want a whole city
made of it the cherubim ask sourly
since it's their comedy routine to be
miserable in this heaven-come-to-earth
where G-d is nowhere to be seen because
G-d has no skin and is too busy giving

"FRESH AIR YOU ARE AN ART STUDENT"

attempting a landscape of the mind or
at least that's what Jackson Pollock does with
your sundress floating on the river's water
it's taken away in an instant and
this is what is meant by "they were naked
and felt no shame" smelling of local
rain acrylic paint and sweat like
"fresh air you are an art student" which
actually means you're a theologian
a boat maker an animal lover
a bird made of popsicle sticks that you
yourself licked though with more compassion in
your eyes than sensuality because
this you said is the true nature of form

THAT OF THE PHARISEES

snow falls from a foreboding syntax
as night excuses itself with the flu
and the dog from next door continues
to bark things perpetually kept from me
down Briar Cliff Street I hate the stars
for their persistence and my lack of love
"a dove is just a symbol" *but also*
just an animal I say in response
to metaphors I find doubtful at thirty
trying to keep a first-time hunger
about me as I walk through the snow
wondering how my righteousness
will ever exceed that of the Pharisees

MOBILE ENOUGH

that G-d's a father how odd to picture
being held back while nothing can
and nothing is holding me Søren
Kierkegaard wrote something like
"at the moment of your deepest suffering
try to relieve the suffering of
others" which sounds impossible but isn't
if one manages to stop writing
poems (which may have already happened)
in order to become a body without
water remaining mobile enough to take
walks around the lake in winter a constant
reminder of the crater at the center

CATHEDRAL

why not listen to Neutral Milk Hotel
as a high school secretary I think
injecting my belly with medication
that refuses to work while writing
these sonnets and taking attendance
answering the phone again and again
to talk with parents about their kids'
delinquencies my father wrestling me
down to the kitchen floor holding
my head under the sink's water
causing me to rise with the glory of
a cathedral enabling me to be baptized
at any moment throughout the day

NO SMALL PREMONITIONS

painting from the thirteenth century
of Eve being pulled from Adam's sleeping
side how lovely you are in lies
small body next to mine the sunlight
streaking across the bedroom ceiling it's
early in the morning and you're wearing
a white tank top waking up to ask me
if a bird just hit the window *no*
I say *why* "because I thought I heard
something sad" you say pushing your hair away
from your face and going back to sleep
leaving me to contemplate the greatness
of a woman who lives mystically and inhabits
the day with no small premonitions

AS YOUR VOICE IS A BOTTLE ROCKET

hello skirmish of bright red fire ants you
nervous bird-herd of the sky jackfruit
painted tie the library leaning back
heavy with ivy under crisscross jet streams
of an empty Doritos bag floating by
with such whimsy it breaks me into thirds
a kind of doxology before this
altar of fire even these streamers
as your voice is a bottle rocket
to me and to everything else simply
a dog whistle (unbearable unhearable)
on the outskirts of campus the prophet waits
scribbling notes about the baby foxes
born just beyond the threshold of the gate

FIGMENT LIKE A FRAGMENT

sunlight in every city is different
due to humidity and other
various factors pollution the voices
of children reflecting off buildings
made of glass rumored to be eternal
like the most violent storm the wind
moving through the street like something
near Galilee the fishermen see
a figment like a fragment on the beach
stoking a fire cooking fish Peter
swims to it and the others follow
like old times except Peter is naked
and Jesus is newly resurrected

"I LAUNCHED A BOAT FRAIL AS A BUTTERFLY"

the naked body my naked body
rheumatoid arthritis and Tylenol
3 my heart beats unseen waves of sunlight
passing through the window next to me I think
through a migraine as stained glass suffering
is a kind of worship at least that's why
I like birds so much so small that you
carried one home in your mitten from
the train it looked sickly and lost when
we let it go and so I promised to make
a bird feeder which I suppose will never
happen now I just can't stop thinking about
that Berrigan sonnet that ends with "sadness
I launched a boat frail as a butterfly"

ALBINO PEAPOD

"the dog's the snow" they say in Sierra Leone
after something such as a chicken or
goat dies "bring it to the moon" they say
hoisting its body up and away and past
the womens' breasts filled with night-light
to the sound of music between them
I stand as a foreigner an albino
peapod sealed up altogether strange
tracing the outline of a circle sketching
a self-portrait with a wooden spoon
on the clay hill where the radio station
stands above the land somehow different when
darkness lifts misunderstanding follows

VODKA IN THE SHOWER

the happenstance of the parallax I
hear a car alarm waking up while you're
in the shower hearing nothing other
than water over brightening freckles
(have you read *Eugene Onegin* in
translation) the branches entering the room
without losing one leaf is what I mean
about parading around nakedly
in the morning's clean light "I should go"
the moth says to the glass of vodka
"no you should stay" the moth imagines
the vodka saying while in reality
there's nothing between the two except
silence and sunlight littered with bees

THE BEAST

the beast who chews the grass gets ahold
of the grass with its blocks-for-teeth inside
the loosely grated sieve of its mind
finds the holy aircraft of the body
sailing through time at a stupid speed
divided by the speed of light in
a street fight between watery brainwaves
and words in a different language said
to slain deer the bears that keeps them here
for way too long the paper-light napkin
collapsing the self into the self infinitely
the shadows of fence posts continually
holding up the grated sieve for the beast

THROUGH A MUTED TRUMPET

passionless I watch the girls strut past
in wool skirts as the business school
lets out down the hall there's a stairwell
I sleep in like an elephant with paper
wings my mind sings through a muted
trumpet its brassy malaise *hurray*
I think to myself *I'm actually writing*
a poem today though it's getting harder
to row around this town's time zone
without wanting to wash the beloved's
hair in the river and then my own
in a moment I'm the deer in the clearing
I'm the hunter I'm the bullet firing

OF COURSE THE DRUMS

walking to Fiona Apple's *The Idler*
Wheel is Wiser than the Driver of the Screw
and Whipping Chords Will Serve You More
than Ropes Will Ever Do the evening's
metal nets and bright bees are removed
from shoreline to the trees where waves break
against themselves like all-too-human
saints unable to slap the sand back down
and be drawn out into the seamless sea
in reverie in Blake-light's last song-sound
as jazz destroyed it all of course the drums
hummed inside the house of the mammal
where I find myself at the thigh of the lake
a pantomime for the rib-hymn's sake

HIPPOPOTAMUS

joyous G-d with a diphthong for a heart
speaking guttural utterances
and finding some soil to dig into
calls man up like a whirlwind from the dust
to name the animals and watch the rain
from within the cleft of a sheltered plane
like all that's real entering in
to the room at once even the windows
are unable to stay shut as the grass
bows down in the eastern breeze it lies
plastered to the ground laughing all the while
"and what do you want to call this little
cloud of dust" *a hippopotamus*
Adam says jokingly though the name sticks

THAT WHICH POINTS AWAY

I have a phantom-limb pain in my tooth
as I walk past the Whole Foods where
the suburbs exist the molar's removed
and a new one's built in its place with
the sudden architecture of a Spanish
mountain mystic's chapel its catacombs
where nerves used to be I see red
brick buildings with dormant ivy climbing
up the gutters and around the windows
in a heliotrope's sun-shaped desire
to continue walking instead of going
home where I have so much to do but will
do nothing or the other way around
in light of that which points away from
the dull persistent pain of what's missing

GLITTER-BOMB
HALLELUJAH

the slow depression of serotonin's
recession before the resurrection
of the heart's intention to continue
like slow snow in the brain love comes
to remind the body of the spirit's
existence whether it's just a breath
or an all out glitter-bomb of a soul
doesn't really matter except that
when I was dying I found myself
alive washing dishes at the kitchen sink
a god-anchor tied to my balloon string
holding me there for the first time
outside the house I grew up inside

A SMALL HILL LIKE A SMALL MOSES

sunlight goes broke as your hand moves
from your hair through the air to your side
where it rests in perfect stasis balancing
the silence inside each unit of sound
obeying neither space nor time you find
a stick on the ground and begin to climb
a small hill like a small Moses though
none of this is real and none of this is
a dream really but rather the result of
a waking vision like the motion of
water following a boat and spreading out
for hours until the shore on either side
receives the tide in such a way that we
speak of all things in terms of happenstance

MORE NAKED THAN EVER DRESSED

moments when G-d's hollow she's a bowl
of caesuras between the shifting snow
flakes and flakes off the monochrome face
choral music's evidence of silence
allowing some snow to gather in her hair
standing there under glass-bulbed Christmas lights
the moon on fire the bottom of the flame
becoming bluer and colder inverting
the expected is quoted throughout winter
in a language of behemoth footprints
leading us closer to frozen forests
under stars hazing our common sense
the landscape more naked than ever dressed

SON OF HOW WAVES ARE SPUN

my thoughts are the arc of your ponytail
perfect and completely meaningless
to the majority of the world
allowing desperation in like a dog
from the cold and breathtaking rain
Technicolor autumn singing songs
to our captors on the muddy banks
of the river we shiver reflective
daughter of someone else and myself
the son of how waves are spun
into shadows together with lichen
and floating algae inside of which
I can see flashes of a fish's body

LIKE A TORTOISE-
SHELL HAIR-CLIP

one hair's width separates forgiveness
in my mind from the daily grind winter's
orange rind on my desk like a torn-up
atmosphere writing these sonnets empty
of everything yet containing all things
the phone rings I don't answer it
grabbing for a pencil with my fingertips
as a tortoise-shell hair-clip grabs hair
CLEAR the medical team screams
pulling the kite of my breathing back down
to what I had before leaving Eden
(a pair of toenail clippers mint soap
blurred vision and a ghost I named G-d)

ELECTRICITY FOR THE SYMPHONY

I felt like the dog who conducted
electricity for the symphony
or the cow who roamed through fields low
as starlight over Mt Olympus the one
Homer saw not the one in Greece I kept
my distance played with the trees in my mind
as if they were hair as if they were
lines radiating continuously unlike
circles which are perpetually
ending the electrical circuits snapping
throughout the storm our whole house plunged
into the darkness that Sappho sung

ST FRANCIS AT THE WEDDING

ducks like winged rockets above the winter
lake charge over a black-branched stand of trees
in the distance a deer falls to its knees
in the snow a crow is watching
everything and nothing at once the moon
visible in the day-lit sky like
a water stain on the mind our eyes align
before behind and within the quiet
St Francis calls the sun small enough
to fit inside the spreading cracks
in the ice as light continues to fall like rice
at a wedding where the bear is marrying
the geometric fish and the trees
are all shouting out "kiss-kiss kiss-kiss"

THE WHOLE GARDEN

my Beatrice touches the trees as she
walks past them with fire ants around her knees
in halos around her kneecaps I snap
in two like a river forking east
to west a sliver of almond between
the teeth of a squirrel I'll keep safe
the image of you happy to do whatever
people used to before the fall
of the oak tree through the middle
of the street (and now the detour of it all)
"nothing with the face of a poet really
which is a flower and not a face with hands
which whisper this is my beloved my"
(and the whole garden will suddenly bow)

OUT OF THE WHIRLWIND

who sways the traffic lights violently
during a suburban rainstorm tell me
if you understand who takes the petals
of spring flowers and makes them livid
funnel clouds around you walking
downtown you must know since you're almost
thirty years old and have contemplated
not one but two birds' bodies so tell me
about the body of a continent
covered in snow in endless nudity
because it's pleasing to me to be
obscene and to fuck with people's ideas
of the holy do you think you're holy
please tell me if you have understanding

UNFOLDING THE NAPKIN

blue snow fell on the behemoth as birds
dove from concrete perches the lips of
buildings *the world's a hungry place* sing
those stars not yet devoured by the collapse
of other stars *what does it sound like inside
a black hole* is like asking what it
sounds like inside the mind can you see it
unfolding the napkin of translucent
thinking is how it was explained to me
this concept that G-d is spirit picture
your own thought as being multi-sided
how many sides can you count now try
to unfold the object until the object
is no longer an object but compassion

NOTIONS OF LOVE

one day I'll die of inspiration
purple finch that I am and forget
to flap my wings on purpose something that
I like to think no one has ever done
before which makes me a person
I suppose presumptuousness coupled
with romantic notions of love
like the unsuspecting crow edging
the building to become a speck of darkness
over a field and away from every
kind of symmetry which I think can be
a kind of inspiration my heart as
I've heard it said "beating like crazy"

WARMER WEATHER

repentance is in assenting to silence
broken by the sound of an airplane I'm
barely holding on to my ill-clad mind
as December comes and goes and time
renews its contract with my toes dug in
to the snow (which I suppose is only
a dare for wanting warmer weather
installing the screen door too early)
yet this poem is going nowhere which is
a metaphor I'm sure as my head is
fucked-up like the bird who flew into
the window breaking its wing and trying
to sing on its way down unsuccessfully

TO LAUGH WILDLY AT HORSE AND RIDER

Job finds himself angry as a blueberry
in the snow outside Grand Rapids
Michigan mid-May where a fresh blight
stays at the center of the whirlwind
and he (the suburbanite) suffers from
a kind of broken vase smashed against
the fireplace flitting ash in leaning
columns of light that expose space
for the chaos it is (the cosmos
it is) as G-d makes remarkably curvy
lines for the sea to forgive the land
knotting the chains of the Pleiades
untying Orion's Belt helping the ostrich
to laugh wildly at horse and rider

FROM THE MOUTH OF GABRIEL

so the angel Gabriel kept his word
and hid his face for my own good he spoke
things I couldn't understand I was
filled with sparks and my joints began
to burn the sky above the interstate
was a needlepoint of my life and I
could finally see how eternity
is not the same thing as forever but
rather an all-at-onceness which makes
time a kind of grace that protects us
from something like the expanse of the sky
or the reality of such a feeling
in a vast field the universe falling
around me like a veil and then lifted

SOLA SCRIPTURA

you're humble and subtle as the slope
of your breasts as singular as a pink
nipple pale as Belgium and England
alike as we lie here drinking table wine
drunk-texting sonnets to whatever
I'd give to smell your hair or bury my
own into the cleft of your collarbone
and then argue with you nakedly in
the morning's light I'd make us some
green tea because I want you healthy
so you can (as the Bible says) continue
to fuck me like a young gazelle

BY THE OTHER SIDE

cathedral made of oyster shells wherein
the pearl both exists and has been
removed I crush white pills into a paste
and use all of them and ingest them
to form the body inside my own
shell of a frame physically depressed
and yoked to death's fluid sculpture
(a Bernini made of birthwater) entering
through a seed-shaped door I pull
at the pant-leg of the Eucharist
a child both spoiled and desperate
the kind of kid who looks through
(and looks to) the stained glass figures
the sunlight enters by the other side

THE LIONS ARE PACING

you have lipstick on your collar I say
to my father the priest that's just the Blood
of Christ my son he replies by and by
(the milky thigh of Mary in my mind)
William Blake's eyes aligning in the snow
a statue outside London simply called
"The Heretic" where birds sit and shit
and live out their days in unconscious praise
of that third space between language
and the mute object sunlight pours through
the stained glass at the Lincoln Park Zoo
where I saw the lions pacing and you
told me to always remember that the cage
is for the protection of the captor

ACKNOWLEDGMENTS

Alice Blue Review, *Arsenic Lobster*, *The Christian Century*, *Corium Magazine*, *Country Music*, *The EcoTheo Review*, *Interrupture*, *Jellyfish*, *Jet Fuel Review*, *Letters*, *Newcity*, *PANK*, *Poetry*, *Sixth Finch*, and *Softblow*.

Eileen Joy, Valerie Vogrin, Michael Snediker, Dean Young, Emily Kendal Frey, Allan Peterson, Rae Armantrout, Douglas Kearney, Simone Muench, Reginald Gibbons, Ed Roberson, Michael Robbins, Anthony Madrid, Sinéad López, Jesús Escobar, Sofia Leiby, Nate Klug, Mel Keiser, Sara Holing, Jacob Comerci, and my family.

Luke Fidler

Matt Opal

*

Laurel and Eleanor

ANTHONY OPAL (b. 1983) is Editor of *The Economy*. His poems can be found in *Poetry*, *Boston Review*, *Harvard Divinity Bulletin*, and elsewhere. He lives near Chicago with his wife and daughter. [anthonyopal.com]

The text of *ACTION* is set in Minion Pro, an original typeface designed by Robert Slimbach in 1990.

Made in the USA
Lexington, KY
13 December 2014